What People Are Saying About

Your DVDs have, without a doubt,
fantastic experience of my entire life... I have screened many "self-help" programs and their comparative effectiveness is not even in the same class. Thank you, Steve!!! They have released my intellect from emotional bondage. *CP*

Your book 'Reiki The Ultimate Guide' seemed to have sought me out and is named well as 'Ultimate'. It is very in depth and contains excellent examples as you explain the process. I especially enjoyed your openness and depth in your describing of Reiki. Your book surpassed any of my expectations and has helped me mentally and physically. I look forward to becoming a Reiki Master and I know with the guidance of your books and DVDs, I can help others too. For that, I thank you dearly. *KD*

I have listened to many music CDs that claimed to help align the chakras or heal emotional and mental scars. This CD is the best I have ever heard! It actually soothed and calmed me after an extremely harrowing day. Each time I use this CD, I find the effects to be better and better. It's truly worth the money. I was able to release my frustration and go on with peace in my heart. *JS*

Steve Murray has hit a home run yet again. I've used all of Steve's Attunement DVDs and guides with very satisfying results. He is a humble, helpful gentleman; even answering all e-mail inquiries personally. In a market glutted with wannabe gurus, messiahs and plastic-enlightened avatars, Steve is an ordinary guy offering genuinely useful information and powerful, yet cost-effective attunements to all. *RD*

I just received your DVDs and books at Christmas. From the moment I started watching the first attunement DVD, my hands heated up and I felt at peace and in tune, even receiving some unrelated psychic information. I love Reiki's ability to transmit to a distant target. This is just the beginning; I know everywhere there are people who have something to offer, but need a bit of healing which I am going to be able to provide thanks to Steve's wonderful work making this magical ability accessible. *LS*

After two years of attending expensive Reiki classes, I discovered Steve Murray's books and DVDs. I was very skeptical at first. I was told Reiki had to be taught in person, distance attunements were not effective, Reiki symbols were secret, it takes years to learn to give Reiki attunements, and many other false beliefs. I purchased Steve's first book and attunement DVD thinking it was a scam, certainly too good to be true. Now, I can't begin to tell you how wrong I was! The first book not only explained everything I had learned in two years, but it also debunked all the false beliefs that Reiki was a long, complicated, and costly process. It also explained how to pass the attunements, which most Reiki masters will not disclose. The attunement DVD was awesome. I will never question the effectiveness of a distance attunement again. I am not a very religious or spiritual person, so if it worked for me, it can work for anyone. Since then, I have purchased all four of Steve's books and all five attunement DVDs. Steve has truly made Reiki available and affordable for everyone! *EM*

The attunements are powerful and the books get right to the point, covering an amazing amount of material in a short time. Without these books, it would take many years of research to learn all of this information. Everything you will ever need to become a Reiki master is packed into these books. Whether you are a beginner or a Reiki master, these books will enhance your abilities. I believe they will be the best investment you will ever make. I wish I had known about Steve's books and DVDs a long time ago. *JV*

The Master & Psychic Attunements work great, plus I saved quite a bit of money in the process. That's perfect, especially for someone who is just starting out. I recommend programs to anyone looking to heal. Thank you, Steve, for enlightening me on my path. *TK*

Reiki has been a blessing to me and has helped bring me out of this overly stressed world that we live in. It truly works and can totally change your life and those who receive Reiki energy through you. For those who aren't believers in Energy Work (I used to be one!), the psychological benefits are amazing. Reiki can truly induce deep relaxation which leads to a healthier body. Thanks, Steve, for the great materials! *DF*

Reiki The Ultimate Guide
Vol. 4

Past Lives & Soul Retrieval
Remove Psychic Debris & Heal Your Life

Steve Murray

First Printing

Body & Mind Productions, Inc.

Reiki The Ultimate Guide Vol. 4
Past Lives & Soul Retrieval
Remove Psychic Debris & Heal Your Life

Published by
Body & Mind Productions
820 Bow Creek Lane, Las Vegas, NV 89134
Website: www.healingreiki.com
Email: bodymindheal@aol.com

First Printing September 2007

Library of Congress Cataloging-in-Publication Data
Murray, Steve
Reiki The Ultimate Guide Vol. 4: Past Lives & Soul Retrieval,
Remove Psychic Debris & Heal Your Life
/ Murray, Steve – 1st ed.
Library of Congress Control Number 2006911044
ISBN # 978-0-9792177-2-2
Includes bibliographical references and index.
1. Reiki 2. New Age 3. Alternative Health
4. Self-Healing 5. Spiritual 6. Healing

Cover design: Paul Melecky, @ ADEXIM Studio, LLC
Type design, production: Dan Berger, @ Bookpack Graphics
Editors: Sonya Baity, Carol von Raesfeld
Illustrations: Paul Melecky, @ ADEXIM Studio, LLC

Printed in U.S.A.

DVDS-CDS-BOOKS

BOOKS by STEVE MURRAY

Cancer Guided Imagery Program
For Radiation, Chemotherapy, Surgery
and Recovery

Stop Eating Junk!
In 5 Minutes a Day for 21 Days

Reiki The Ultimate Guide
Learn Sacred Symbols and Attunements
Plus Reiki Secrets You Should Know

Reiki The Ultimate Guide Vol. 2
Learn Reiki Healing with Chakras
plus New Reiki Healing Attunements
for All Levels

Reiki The Ultimate Guide Vol. 3
Learn New Reiki Aura Attunements
Heal Mental and Emotional Issues

Reiki False Beliefs Exposed
For All Misinformation
Kept Secret by a Few Revealed

Reiki The Ultimate Guide Vol. 4
Past Lives & Soul Retrieval
Remove Psychic Debris & Heal your Life

DVDS by STEVE MURRAY

Reiki Master Attunement
Become a Reiki Master

Reiki 1st Level Attunement
Give Healing Energy to Yourself
and Others

Reiki 2nd Level Attunement
Learn and Use the Reiki Sacred
Symbols

Reiki Psychic Attunement
Open and Expand Your Psychic
Abilities

A Reiki 1st
Aura and Chakra
Attunement Performed

Reiki Healing Attunement
Heal Emotional-Mental-
Physical-Spiritual Issues

Successfully Preparing for Cancer
Radiation A Guided Imagery
and Subliminal Program

Preparing Mentally & Emotionally
For Cancer Chemotherapy
A Guided Imagery Program

Preparing Mentally & Emotionally
For Cancer Surgery
A Guided Imagery Program

Lose Fat and Weight
Stop Eating Junk!
In 5 minutes A Day for 21 Days

How To Contact Angels and
Departed Love Ones
A Step By Step Guide

Fear and Stress Relief
Subliminal Program
Let Your Unconscious Mind Do It!

Preparing Mentally & Emotionally
For Cancer Radiation
A Guided Imagery Program

Pain Relief Subliminal Program
Let Your Unconscious Mind Do It!

Destroying Cancer Cells
Guided Imagery and Subliminal
Program

30-Day Subliminal Weight Loss
Program Let Your Unconscious
Mind Do the Work!

Stop Smoking Using Your
Unconscious Mind
A Subliminal Program

Successfully Preparing for Cancer
Chemotherapy A Guided Imagery
and Subliminal Program

CDS by STEVE MURRAY

Reiki Healing Music
Attunement: Volume One

Reiki Healing Music
Attunement: Volume Two

Reiki Psychic Music
Attunement: Volume One

Reiki Psychic Music
Attunement: Volume Two

Reiki Aura Music Attunement

Reiki Chakra Music Attunement

Cancer Fear and Stress Relief Program

DVDS by BODY & MIND PRODUCTIONS

Learning to Read the Tarot
Intuitively

Learning to Read the Symbolism
of the Tarot

This book is dedicated to

Wei and Joyce Murray

Steve's Reiki Mission Statement

To make Reiki knowledge, guidance and Attunements available to everyone that seeks them. To make Reiki 1st, 2nd and Master Level Attunements affordable for everyone, so healing can be spread throughout the world.

Steve Murray

CONTENTS

Creation is all space, all time - all things past, present, and future.

- Matthew Fox

The Journey Begins

The past, the present and the future are really one: they are today.

- Harriet Beecher Stowe

Introduction

Before You Begin

Welcome to the fourth book in the Reiki Ultimate Guide series. This book will show you how to perform a Past Life and Soul Retrieval Session. The methods you will learn can be used with or without Reiki.

However, I believe the sessions and results are enhanced when Reiki is used. If you have not been attuned to Reiki, perhaps this will give you an incentive to do so.

The first Ultimate Guide in the series includes step-by-step instructions on how to perform all the Reiki Level Attunements — 1st, 2nd, and Master. The guide also has steps for a Reiki Psychic and Healing Attunement. The second Ultimate Guide is devoted to Reiki and the Chakras. It includes a formula for Reiki Chakra Healing Attunements for any ailment and disease in the physical body. The third Ultimate Guide shows how to work with Reiki and the Aura with step-by-step instructions for specific Aura Attunements for mental, emotional and spiritual issues.

Why learn methods for experiencing a Past Life or Soul Retrieval when you have all the healing options taught in the first three Reiki books? There are several answers. One, as explained in all of the previous Reiki Ultimate Guides, healing options are needed for different people, situations and circumstances. And, that can change with each healing session. For example, a person might need a Reiki Chakra Healing Attunement for arthritis pain during one session and the next session a Reiki Aura Attunement for anger to clear up the root cause of the arthritis. You need to have different healing options for the physical, mental, emotional and spiritual bodies for optimum results with healing.

Two, at times you may need a breakthrough with healing in order to make the Reiki Attunements taught in the first Reiki books more effective. The breakthrough is in releasing and then destroying stubborn Psychic Debris that is in the Aura or Chakras. A Past Life and/or a Soul Retrieval Session are invaluable for achieving this.

When Psychic Debris in the mental, emotional, spiritual, or physical body is released and destroyed, your life force (Reiki) can start to return to its normal healthy flow. This makes all subsequent healing work more effective. In fact, some Healers prefer to perform these sessions with their clients before any other healing work is done. Or, they combine it with early healing sessions. The good news is usually only one or two sessions of a Past Life or Soul Retrieval are needed for a Psychic Debris breakthrough, and the results can often be felt and/or seen immediately. After the breakthrough, you can continue with Reiki Aura or Chakra Healing Attunements.

Now let's define "Psychic Debris."

Psychic Debris

Psychic Debris is referred to by many different names, which include "negative thought forms" and "emotional or mental blocks." Whatever it's called, most Healers are aware of it and agree that this phenomenon exists.

Psychic Debris can manifest as phobias, anger, fears, grief, anxiety or stress and can negatively affect your life. Psychic Debris eventually accumulates in some or all of your bodies - physical, mental, emotional and spiritual, thus creating blockages of your life force. The first place Psychic Debris usually manifests is in the mental, emotional and spiritual bodies in the Aura. If it is not released from

15

the Aura and subsequently destroyed, it will eventually resonate down to and affect your physical body. This can cause a weakening of your immune system, resulting in illness and disease.

One of the primary sources that create Psychic Debris is unprocessed emotions. Emotions will accumulate over a period of time if they are not processed or released by the individual during the event(s) or circumstance(s) in a timely manner. Normally these emotions (fear, grief, anger, hate, etc.) are necessary for the events and circumstances at the time they are generated. Processed and released in a timely manner, emotions are not negative but just a necessary part of the human experience for survival and healing. When unprocessed emotions are held onto by the conscious or unconscious mind and not processed and released, they can accumulate in and around a person's body (Aura and Chakras) and manifest into Psychic Debris. This is when wellness challenges commence.

Another way Psychic Debris is created is by reliving unresolved life experience(s) repeatedly, remembering instances with great detail and emotion. These experiences have a negative emotional charge linked to them. The charge can be anger, fear, anxiety, etc., so when a person mentally relives the unresolved experience, it sets off this negative emotional charge[1], which creates Psychic Debris. Unresolved life experienc relived in the mind can be anything a person perceives as such. A few examples might be: not speaking up for yourself at work, not saying your peace to a loved one before death, a divorce with

---

[1] An emotional charge is a strong emotional reaction to a circumstance, person, place or thing.

loose ends, an argument that's left open-ended or not showing up for a funeral. Ultimately, Psychic Debris can be different for many individuals. It can be caused by many sources and circumstances unique to the person's life experience, current and past. Performing a Past Life or Soul Retrieval Session will help release and remove Psychic Debris created from any source from the past.

Soul

Throughout this book, I use the word "Soul." The definition or concept of a Soul varies between teachers, authors, dictionaries, religions and metaphysical teachings. To compound matters, "Soul" is also interchanged with "Spirit" in everyday language and conversations. Spirit and Soul are synonyms in many thesauri, and dictionaries cross-reference definitions between the two words. Soul is a very subjective term and its meaning and definition are based on your own beliefs and experiences. There is no need to get distracted by a philosophical discussion about what a Soul is or the difference of Soul versus Spirit. You can keep your own definition, belief or concept of the Soul. In fact, some healers refer to Soul Retrieval as "Spirit Retrieval," and that's okay. The methods you will learn for a Soul Retrieval Session will still be effective no matter your own personal beliefs about the Soul.

A common ground for the meaning or the concept of the soul is this -- people and cultures today and throughout history have felt that there is an essence in humans that goes beyond the physical body and mind. In other words, the common belief is that there is "another element" to a person besides the body and mind.

Time

During a Past Life or Soul Retrieval Session, you access memories from another time. So, let's talk about time, or to be more specific, chronological time. Chronological time is a widely held theory. It is believed that all time and events move forward in a linear fashion, and it is defined by many chronological methods that include ticking clocks and calendars. The belief of chronological time establishes continuity in our minds in processing and communicating the vast information we receive and process by our senses. It also gives us equilibrium by keeping us from perceiving all things at once.

The reality is that a working theory of chronological time is needed for most of us to live our daily lives. However, by studying black holes[2] in space, physicists and astronomers have started to discover that the theory of chronological time is not so clear-cut — that time is not chronological, but fluid and flexible. Of course, metaphysics teachings have stated for centuries that all time in the universe is not chronological at all. That, in fact, all time and events are layered and occurring simultaneously, the past, present and future in different dimensions (Illus. 1).

If you have belief in chronological time being absolute, you will need to suspend it or at the very least keep an open mind during a Past Life or Soul Retrieval Session. If you are reading this book now, I suspect you are already open

---

[2] An area in space that has such a strong gravitational pull that no matter or energy can escape from it. The black hole event horizon is the boundary that, once past it, nothing can escape from the black hole. It is theorized that time will slow down as one approaches a black hole, and because of its infinite density, it causes all time and space to be the same.

Illus. 1

to the idea of time and events being fluid and flexible. If you already embrace the concept of all time and events occurring simultaneously, then experiencing a Past Life or Soul Retrieval Session will reinforce this belief.

**Never run away from the past,
face it and learn from it**.

\- Linda Woolverton

The past is a guide post, not a hitching post.

- L. Thomas Holdcroft

Akashic Records

Akashic Defined

One of the main elements in a Past Life or Soul Retrieval session is accessing and viewing past memories. These memories are known as the "Akashic Records." The Akashic Records store all the events of all lives (including the current) that have existed since the beginning of man and are located in a dimension I call the "Akashic Plane."

Akashic is a Sanskrit word meaning "sky", "space" or "ether." The word Akasha, from which "Akashic" is derived, combines two Tibetan words: "Aka," which translates into space, storage or repository, and "Sa," which can be used to mean sky, secret or hidden. One translation for the Akashic Records that I like is, "a library of hidden records." Many cultures[3] throughout history have used the Akashic Records in healing. The earliest mention of this concept in traceable history is about 7500 BCE.

The most famous person to bring recognition to Akashic Records in the modern era was Edgar Cayce[4]. He accessed the records to help people heal or with other life challenges.

Accessing the Records

I believe there is a counterpart that a normal person cannot see (although some psychics can) that exists alongside the physical body. This counterpart is the spiritual, ether[5] double of the physical body and is commonly called the "Astral Body" (Illus. 2). Some teachings referred to it as the "Etheric Double."

Like the word "Soul," *Astral Body* has many interpretations in metaphysics. But, no matter what the teachings about the Astral Body are, it is acknowledged that there is an ether-

---

[3] Tibetans, Egyptians, Persians, Greeks, Chinese, Hebrews, Christians, Druids, and Mayans, to name a few...

[4] Born March 18, 1877, died January 3, 1945. He was known as "The Sleeping Prophet", and he was famous for going into a meditative state and accessing what he called the Hall of Records (i.e., Akashic Records) and helping people with medical problems.

[5] Aether, æther or ether in metaphysics is the main component of what everything non-physical is made of, including the Aura.

like double or template that contains all the consciousness (i.e., emotions, thoughts, memories, etc.) that mirrors the physical body. This double or template can travel across time and to different planes (dimensions) of existence under the right conditions.

During a Past Life and/or a Soul Retrieval Session, you set up the right conditions for your Astral Body to access the Akashic Plane and the Akashic Records. This is accomplished by following my methods in a relaxed state, using visualization, imagination and your conscious and subconscious mind simultaneously.

Methods

There are a variety of methods taught to reach the Akashic Plane and access the Akashic Records. All start with a process to ease into a relaxed state at the beginning. After being guided into a relaxed state, some methods have you visualizing going up stairs, elevators, floating in large balloons or traveling imagined timelines to reach the Akashic Plane. Others might have you going down[6] stairs or elevators to reach the Plane. Once arriving at the Akashic Plane, you may or may not have guides meeting you to access the Akashic Records. The records are in huge libraries or temples, stored in books and/or scrolls for you to read what you need to know and understand.

---

[6] I personally do not like any visualization method that has you going down in any way, shape, or form due to the unconscious reference or conscious connotation of hell.

Illus. 2

No matter how complicated the methods, if followed, all should work to a certain degree. In reality, you have the capability to use any method, including your own to access the Akashic Plane and Records. The challenge is if a person is successful in accessing the plane and records, what's next? The majority of people need a structured template for a Past Life or Soul Retrieval Session to access the Akashic Plane and Records. And once there, what is most vital is having guidance on what to do next.

You will find the methods I teach for a Past Life or Soul Retrieval Session give complete guidance from the beginning of the session to the end of the session. Plus, they are easy to perform and streamlined compared to others. Streamlined in the sense that I developed the methods to be specific and used for therapeutic purposes only, nothing more.

Also, other methods might have you spend a lot of time exploring, a past life in all its aspects, including the moment of death. With Soul Retrieval, many methods include a lot of ritual in the process. I believe this is not necessary for a Past Life and Soul Retrieval to be successful.

In closing this chapter I would like to say, I do not recommend using any method (including my own) for performing a Past Life or Soul Retrieval Session for fun or to satisfy a person's curiosity. There is always a possibility that the information obtained under these circumstances could add unnecessary mental clutter, Psychic Debris, and confusion to the present life. So why risk it?

Who controls the past controls the future.

- George Orwell

Visual and Non-Visual

Perceiving the Past

Before you perform a Past Life or Soul Retrieval Session, you need to know if you are a visual or non-visual person and follow a few suggestions. Let's start with finding out if you are visual or non-visual.

Visual or non-visual is the mode the person will be in when visualizing during a Past Life or Soul Retrieval Session.

Being visual is being able to close your eyes and see pictures and images in your mind's eye (Illus. 3). With these pictures, some people can also hear sounds and voices, detect smells, and can feel an emotional charge linked to the pictures and images. The combination of this can vary with a visual person, but all visual people will see images or pictures with their eyes closed. The majority of people are visual.

Some people have difficulty seeing images or pictures or cannot see them at all when they close their eyes. These people are non-visual. However, this group is very kinesthetic[7] and will be able to sense and even describe images and pictures even though they cannot visualize them in their mind. Some non-visual people can also hear sounds and voices, detect smells and feel the emotional charge linked to what they are experiencing in a non-visual mode.

Why is it important to know if a person is visual or non-visual? If you are visual, you realize you will see images and pictures during a Past Life or Soul Retrieval Session without a problem. If you discover you are non-visual, you will understand why and not be disappointed that you are not able to see pictures and/or images during a Past Life or Soul Retrieval Session. The bottom line is this: even if you are a non-visual person, you can still have a session which is just as effective as that of a visual person.

---

[7] Able to feel, sense or know with the mind without visual feedback.

Illus. 3

It is interesting to note that some of the strongest psychics are non-visual. They receive their information from feelings and a knowing, without pictures or images. If you are a non-visual person, you are in good company.

Keep in mind, when I refer to visualizing throughout the book, it is in reference to the way you personally are able to do it, visual or non-visual.

Visual or Non-Visual Test

You can take the following simple test to find out if you are visual or non-visual.

Close your eyes. Imagine being at a favorite place. This can be outdoors, a friend's house, the gym, parent's house, etc. Now, while you are imagining this place, can you see your surroundings? If so, describe what you see.

If you cannot see what you are imagining, describe it anyway. You will find that although you cannot visualize the favorite place, you can still describe it. If you are able to see the favorite place, you are visual; if you are only able to describe it, you are non-visual.

Suggestions

Next are suggestions to follow prior to a Past Life or Soul Retrieval Session. If not all of the suggestions can be followed, just do as many as possible.

➢ Limit or stop eating all animal protein six hours before the session.

➢ Consume only water or juice four to six hours before the session.
➢ Limit or discontinue caffeine consumption four to six hours before the session.
➢ No alcohol for at least 24 hours before the session.
➢ Limit sugar 12 hours before the session.
➢ Limit or stop smoking four to six hours before the session.

Following the suggestions will increase your conscious mind's clarity and focus during a session. Additionally, these suggestions help your physical body get into a relaxed state more easily and quickly, which is necessary for a successful session.

We can draw lessons from the past, but we cannot live in it.

- Lyndon B. Johnson

Preparations

Ground and Clear

There are two steps of preparation you need to do before performing every Past Life or Soul Retrieval Session. They are grounding yourself and clearing the area where the session will be performed.

Grounding

A person should always ground him or herself prior to a Past Life or Soul Retrieval Session. This ensures the person will be balanced and focused during the entire session. Experienced Healers usually have their own methods and processes for doing this and should feel free to use them.

One simple and effective way to do this is to stand and take a moment to bring Reiki[8] through the top of the head (7th Chakra) all the way down through the body, then out both legs into the earth (Illus. 4). Wait a few seconds, then bring it back from the earth, all the way back up both legs and out the top of the head (Illus. 5). This whole process should only take a few minutes and there is usually a sense or feeling of balance after the process is complete. Again, you can use your own method as long as it grounds you before a session.

Clearing

Doing one or more of the following suggestions will clear and remove any Psychic Debris that might already be present in the area where the session will be performed. Just like a surgeon wants a germ-free environment when he or she operates to avoid infections, you need a Psychic Debris-free environment when performing a session. If the room is not cleared, any lingering Psychic Debris in the room can attach to your Aura or Chakras at a vulnerable moment during a session and could cause unforeseen problems.

---

[8] If you're not a Reiki Healer, just visualize healing energy or universal life force.

Illus. 4

Illus. 5

Make sure your intent is to clear the room of any Psychic Debris while performing any of the following suggestions:

➢ Visualize or imagine white or golden light filling the area where the session will be performed
➢ Smudge or sage the room
➢ Place Reiki Crystals or Reiki Healing Stones in the corners of the room
➢ Draw Reiki Symbols and activate them in all corners of the room.

Those who cannot remember the past are condemned to repeat it.

- George Santayana

Relaxation Techniques

Two Techniques

I begin each Past Life or Soul Retrieval Session with a relaxation technique. The following are two you can use. Both techniques are simple, easy to learn, and only take about two minutes from start to finish.

The first technique is for a visual person, although a non-visual person definitely can use it. A non-visual person using this technique will feel and sense the sphere of light that is used as it moves throughout the physical body. The second technique is for a non-visual person, but a visual person can use it also.

These two Relaxation Techniques will not place you into a deep meditation or put you to sleep. They are designed to quickly ease the body, then the mind, into a state of light relaxation. When you are in this light state of relaxation, it is easier to access the Akashic Plane.

I recommend practicing the technique of your choice several times before doing an actual Past Life or Soul Retrieval Session so that you will be accustomed to using it.

Relaxation Technique One

1. You are sitting in a comfortable chair with your hands face down in your lap. Your legs can be crossed yoga style (Illus. 6) or uncrossed.

2. Take five slow, deep breaths and then visualize a radiating sphere of golden or white healing light on top of your Crown Chakra (Illus. 7). You are going to move this orb of healing light throughout your physical body and while doing so, you will imagine it releasing healing light and relaxing your body.

Illus. 6

Illus. 7

3. Let the sphere flow into your Crown Chakra, down into your neck, where it will pause (Illus. 8); take a deep breath.

4. Next, have the sphere of light travel toward your left shoulder, all the way down your left arm to your left hand, where it pauses (Illus. 9); take a deep breath.

5. After the breath, have the sphere travel back up your arm to your right shoulder, down your right arm, where it pauses in your right hand (Illus. 10); take a deep breath.

6. After the breath, visualize the sphere traveling back up your right arm and shoulder to your neck, where it pauses (Illus. 11); take a deep breath.

7. After the breath, have the sphere flow to the Heart Chakra, where it pauses (Illus. 12); take a deep breath.

8. After the breath, have the sphere flow to the Root Chakra (Illus. 13), pause; take a deep breath.

9. After the breath, have the sphere flow toward your left hip, all the way down your left leg, where it pauses at your left foot (Illus. 14); take a deep breath.

10. After the breath, have the sphere come all the way back up the left leg, through the hip, back to the Root Chakra, and toward the right hip, down the right leg, until it pauses at your right foot (Illus. 15); take a deep breath.

Illus. 8

Illus. 9

Illus. 10

Illus. 11

Illus. 12

Illus. 13

Illus. 14

Illus. 15

11. After the breath, have the sphere flow back up your right leg and hip, through the Root Chakra, all the way up through the Heart Chakra, neck, then all the way out through the Crown Chakra where it dissolves (Illus. 16).

You are now in a relaxed state. Take a moment before you start the session.

Relaxation Technique Two

1. You are sitting in a comfortable chair with your eyes closed and your hands face down in your lap. Your legs can be crossed (yoga style) or uncrossed.

2. Take five easy, deep breaths, focusing on really filling up the lungs. On each exhale, quietly or silently say the word "relax." When you are done with the five breaths, just resume your normal breathing and stop saying the word "relax."

3. Next, with your eyes still closed, simultaneously tense or tighten your entire upper body as best you can: arms, chest, neck, hands, etc. Tightening your upper body might seem awkward at first for some people, but with practice, you will soon become an expert at it. Keep your upper body tense (Illus. 17) for about 30 seconds, then release the tension and let your upper body relax and go limp for 30 seconds. While you are doing this, just continue to breathe at your own pace.

Illus. 16

Illus. 17

4. With your eyes still closed, simultaneously tense or tighten your entire lower body the best you can: hips, legs, calves, feet, etc. Keep your lower body tense (Illus. 18) for 30 seconds, then release the tension and let your lower body relax and go limp for 30 seconds. After that, take three more deep breaths.

Now the entire body is in a relaxed state (Illus. 19). Take a moment before you start the session.

Guidelines

Now that you have a learned two relaxation techniques, there are just a few guidelines you need to know before performing a Past Life or Soul Retrieval Session, and they are:

➤ A Past Life or Soul Retrieval Session has to be performed in a quiet, peaceful place where you will be completely undisturbed.

➤ The length of a session can vary from thirty minutes to forty-five minutes, or longer. The time all depends on the person and the time they need personally to complete all the steps in a session.

➤ Eyes should be closed during a session and light meditation music can be played at a low volume in the background.

➤ Wear loose clothing and sit in a comfortable chair in a relaxed posture.

Illus. 18

Illus. 19

➢ Trying to force something to happen during a Past Life or Soul Retrieval Session doesn't really work well; in fact, it can delay the process. So take your time during each step in a session. And, it is important that you do not proceed to the next step until the step you are on has been completed.

Okay, you have now learned two Relaxation Techniques and guidelines for a Past Life and Soul Retrieval Session. In the next segments of the book you will learn how to perform both.

The more anger towards the past you carry in your heart, the less capable you are of loving the present.
- Barbara De Angelis

Take time to gather up the past so that you will be able to draw from your experience and invest them in the future.

- Jim Rohn

Past Lives

Change is not merely necessary to life - it is life.

- Alvin Toffler

Reincarnation

Reincarnation Defined

If I am going to talk about past lives, I need to first discuss reincarnation. You cannot have a past life without it. Reincarnation, also called "rebirth," means "to come again in the flesh." Reincarnation is a belief system that is embraced by many cultures and religions throughout the world. Its earliest roots come from the Hindu-Buddhist religious beliefs of the perpetual birth-death-birth cycle (Illus. 20), where a Soul moves from body to body. In fact, early Christians were believers in reincarnation. The common thread among the various beliefs regarding reincarnation is that upon death, the Soul exits the body, then begins to prepare to come back into life within another body, and then does so.

The circumstances of each time a Soul returns to a new body are determined by the growth and goals achieved in the previous lives, as well as what needs to be accomplished in the next life. It is believed the process of reincarnation continues until the Soul has reached a state of perfection and merges back with its source (God).

The Veil

Why don't we remember all our past lives each time we are born? We are shielded from the memories of past lives because the thoughts, images, traumas and experiences would overwhelm us in our present life. We would not be able to focus on what needs to be done in the present life. This shielding is commonly referred to as the *veil*. The veil is not as strong with the young. Children may remember a great deal of past life information, but they are usually discouraged from talking about these recollections, and they soon forget them as they grow older and move on in life. There are many documented[9] cases of children recalling verifiable facts and figures of history, with no plausible explanation as to how they acquired this information, except for having had a past life.

Illus. 20

As adults, occasionally the veil is lifted and glimpses of past lives are revealed. Although, when this happens, most people just shrug the experience off and give no significant after-thought to its meaning.

Déjà Vu

The most common experience of the veil being lifted is known as "déjà vu." This French expression translates as "already seen." However, the commonly understood meaning of *déjà vu* is usually lumped together with three other déjà definitions: *déjà visite*, which means "already visited," *déjà vécu*, which means "already experienced or lived through," and *déjà senti*, which means "already felt." So, when we describe déjà vu (even though it might actually be one or a combination of the other three déjàs) we are referring to the feeling of having visited a place or experienced a certain sensation or sequence of events before - like recognizing a street or house as being vaguely familiar, even though it has never been visited before. Déjà vu can also be experienced when meeting a new person; there may exist a sense of familiarity, a history with the person, even though consciously you know that you have never had any contact with that person before.

Déjà vu is not the only way fragments of past-life memories surface from the veil. On occasion, memories come forth briefly in recurring dreams, triggered by a trauma, terrifying incident, watching a movie, viewing an old

---

[9] Dr. Ian Stevenson, for example, is one of many who have researched into the past lives of children. He is the author of *Children Who Remember Previous Lives* and has documented over a 40-year period more than 2,600 cases that show "undeniable evidence" for children remembering past lives.

painting or reading a book. These instances may briefly and spontaneously occur at any time, but with a Past Life Session, you are able to lift the veil for a longer period of time and control the sequence for more clarity.

Questions

The following is a list of typical questions, although not all-inclusive, that can give an indication of a past life. Take a few moments and answer them.

➢ Are there places in the world you have always wanted to visit?
➢ Are there places in the world you have a fear of visiting?
➢ Are there segments of history to which you are drawn?
➢ Are there activities in which you have always wanted to participate?
➢ Are there activities you have always wanted to avoid?
➢ Are there any groups (religious, political, etc.) you are attracted to or maybe avoid?
➢ Are there fears or phobias that you have had since childhood for no apparent reason?
➢ Do you have natural talents or abilities that don't run in your family?
➢ Are there any unexplained chronic health problems and/or emotional issues in your life?
➢ Are there people you have felt instantly close to, even if you have not known them long?
➢ Are there people you have felt uncomfortable being around for no apparent reason?

Now that you have answered the questions, maybe you are surprised how some answers do not have a basis, connection or source in your present life. In fact, the answers give indications or clues to past lives.

Are Past Lives Real?

Mainstream society dismisses anything that does not fit its perception of reality by saying, "It's just your imagination..." So, the question often arises, are the memories accessed during a Past Life Session real? Any memories a person has are real to that individual.

The fact is, not one person can judge another person's memories as false. To this day, there is no proof that past lives do not exist, but there have been many researched cases turned into books[10] on past life memories. These cases proved to be historically accurate; some include verification of a specified person existing at the stated period in time.

If you have concerns or mental blocks about the memories of a Past Life Session being authentic, simply treat them like a metaphor for your current life situation. By applying the knowledge and wisdom learned from this metaphor, you will still be able to gain positive results from the session.

The truth of the matter is this -- it really doesn't matter if your past life memories are real to other people. What's important is the Past Life Session helps you help yourself.

---

[10] See selected Bibliography for books on the topic.

The past is behind, learn from it.
The future is ahead, prepare for it.
The present is here, live it

- Thomas S. Monson

The past has to inform the present.

- John Turturro

Past Life Root Event

Root Event Defined

A Past Life Root Event is a traumatic incident in a person's past life that has created a negative emotional charge. The negative emotional charge is carried forward to succeeding lives. This negative emotional charge is then responsible for specific problems that manifest Psychic Debris in one's present life.

I believe the negative emotional charge is carried forward from the past life for two reasons. The event may have happened suddenly[11], and there was no time to process the emotions and understand what happened. Or, the event was so traumatic, the mind went into denial at the time of the event, which prevented processing the emotions and understanding what took place.

With all the past lives a person can have, I would imagine there are hundreds of Root Events that can have negative emotional charges linked to them. But, only one negative emotional charge from a specific root cause will carry over and affect a present life. Why is this? And, why does this not occur at all for many people? I can't give a definitive answer (nobody can). My guess is it has to do with Karma[12] and/or learning or not learning a lesson from the Past Life Root Event, with the lessons not learned being the main reason emotional charges from a Past Life Root Event surface in a present life.

The good news is, if a negative emotional charge has been carried over to your present life and is causing problems, I can teach you how to perform a Past Life Session. This will release it, thus clearing up Root Event problems.

Root Event Problems

Here's a list of a few possible problems in a present life that could have manifested from a Root Event that was created in a Past Life.

---

[11] Such as sudden death, like a drowning, fatal fall, murder, etc.

[12] Karma is the total effect of a person's actions and conduct during the successive phases of the person's existence and regarded as determining the person's destiny or fate.

➤ Unexplained acute pains
➤ Chronic pain
➤ Health syndromes
➤ Illness and disease
➤ Phobias
➤ Bad habits
➤ Weight issues
➤ Relationship issues
➤ Love issues
➤ Mental and emotional blocks
➤ Unexplained fear
➤ Harmful behavior that is repeated

Past Life Session

The Past Life process you will learn in the next chapter is my method to enter the Akashic Plane. Once there, you can access the Akashic Records and review the memory of the past life where the Root Event that is responsible for causing the challenge in the present life first manifested. Once the memory of the Root Event is observed, you are able to understand how and why the negative emotional charge was created. Typically, the insight (learning) will instantly release the negative emotional charge from this past life event and present life. The release will be like a domino effect through all previous lives forward to the present life where it was creating problems and Psychic Debris.

For example, maybe you now have a hard time taking commands from authority figures, which results in conflicts and Psychic Debris. Upon observing a past life memory, you discover that you held the role of a high authority and were used to giving the orders, not taking them. But, this authority was lost (Root Event) and you were devastated, thus creating a negative emotional charge.

With this insight, the emotional charge is instantly released in the past life memory and current life. With this release, conflicts of authority start to resolve themselves, and Psychic Debris is released in the present life.

Points to Remember

Before moving on to the next chapters on performing a Past Life Session, there a few important points you should remember:

➢ In a past life memory, your gender and, of course, your appearance can change, but you will always recognize yourself. In addition, you might recognize people who are important to you in the present life playing different roles in a past life. For example, a person who was your brother in a past life can be your mother, boss or best friend in the present life. The relationships and gender of these people can be different, but they will be recognizable. If this happens, you will view your present relationships with these people with more understanding.

➢ Whether a visual or non-visual person, consciousness is never lost during a session and both are capable of speaking during a session if guided[13] by another.

---

[13] See Chapter 14 on guiding a session.
.

➢ The experiences a person can have during a Past Life Session are varied and it can change from session to session. As previously mentioned, the type of experience is also based on whether you are a visual or non-visual person.

➢ A past life memory can provide precise or piecemeal information. Regardless of how much information is provided, it will always be enough to make the Past Life Session beneficial and successful.

Do not dwell in the past, do not dream of the future,
concentrate the mind on the present moment.

- Buddha

Past Life Seven Segments

Guidance

In this chapter, I will explain and guide you through each of the seven segments of a Past Life Session. In the following chapter, I will take you through a sample Past Life Session step-by-step with illustrations, so the process will be easy to perform the first time.

Seven Segments

➢ Preparation
➢ Starting the session
➢ Relaxation technique
➢ Entering the Akashic Plane
➢ Root Event insight
➢ Leaving the Akashic Plane
➢ Clearing Psychic Debris

Okay, let's talk about what needs to be done in each segment. If you are not a Reiki Healer, omit all the steps that require drawing[14] and activating[15] Reiki Symbols. Just bypass these steps and go to the next step that does not have Reiki Symbols involved.

Preparation

Do all the preparation steps as outlined in Chapter 4, which include grounding yourself and clearing the room. This should be completed before beginning a session.

Starting the Session

Sit in a quiet, peaceful place where you will be undisturbed for the entire Past Life Session. At this time, as an option, you can ask your Source, Higher Self, Guides, Guardian Angels, etc., to help and/or give guidance during the session. Again, this is only an option and is not required.

---

[14] There are many methods Reiki Healers use to draw a Reiki Symbol. Visualizing and tracing the symbols in the air are just a few. Whichever method you were taught is the method you should use.

[15] To activate a Reiki Symbol means to "turn it on," "make it work," "go into action," etc.

Now, draw and activate the Power Symbol in front of the sixth chakra (Third Eye), then visualize it going into this chakra. This will help increase your awareness and psychic abilities during the session.

Next, draw and activate the Mental/Emotional Symbol in front of the fourth chakra (Heart Chakra), then visualize it going into the Heart Chakra. This will help with the emotional process and emotional aspects of the session.

Now, silently state the intention for the Past Life Session to yourself. For example, "I am going to discover the Root Event in my past life that is responsible for my migraine headaches." Use your own phrasing to make it personal and truly intentional.

Relaxation Technique

Next, perform one of the relaxation techniques explained in Chapter Five. Either one will work. If you have your own relaxation technique that will not make you fall asleep, use it.

Entering the Akashic Plane

You are now in a relaxed state. Visualize in front of you an almost blinding white or golden light filling the room from ceiling to floor, slowly spinning, and forming the shape of a Vortex. Take a few moments to view the Vortex.

Now, draw and activate the Long Distance Symbol before you, then visualize it going into the Vortex. This will help with going into and returning from the Akashic Plane.

If you are a Reiki Master, do the same with the Master Symbol. Draw and activate it, then visualize the symbol going into the Vortex. This helps increase the overall clarity of the experience in the Akashic Plane.

Next, visualize getting up and walking into the middle of this Vortex. After a few seconds, you will exit the Vortex on the other side into the Akashic Plane, a place that is endless and ever-expanding.

In front of you is a flowing grey wall that extends out in all directions as far as you can see, to infinity. You understand the wall is impregnable and represents a veil.

On the wall[16] will be one lone porthole at eye level. The porthole is shaped like one you would see on a ship and it's made out of a glass-like substance. Beyond this porthole is the past life memory with the Root Event you need to view, the reason you entered the Akashic Plane.

Root Event Insight

Take a few moments, then when you are ready, walk up to and look in the porthole. Looking through the porthole, you might see images right away or there might be a light, foggy mist, or even darkness. If this happens, keep looking; slowly, images of the past life memory will appear. Image(s) might be in natural colors or black and white. There is no significance to the color of the memory, so do not worry if it is in black and white.

---

[16] The wall will also protect you from any additional Psychic Debris that might be in the past life memory.

There are at least two ways that you may view the Root Event as you are looking through the porthole. You might see images like a short movie and it will play only once, or it will play a few times. Another possibility is that you will just see one image that tells the whole story of the Root Event. In whatever form the past life memory appears (images or a single image), you observe in a focused manner, utilizing all your senses to gather all the necessary information.

While observing the past life memory of the Root Event, you will understand how and why the negative emotional charge manifested from this event. Once this insight[17] occurs, instantly, the emotional charge that is in the Root Event and linked to your present life will be released from both lives, past and present.

As mentioned in Chapter 7, the release will be like a domino effect through all previous lives forward to the present life where it was creating problems and Psychic Debris. At this time, Psychic Debris will also be released from the Aura and Chakras, which will start the process of healing for the problem(s) in the present life.

The length of time it will take to gain this insight depends on the person and the magnitude of the Root Event. Usually, it takes from a few seconds to a few minutes, but it can take longer in some instances. You cannot proceed to the next step until the insight is acquired, so take as much time as needed to gain the insight.

---

[17] Insight: A clear or deep perception of a situation or circumstance; understanding the inward or hidden nature of things.

Leaving the Akashic Plane

Now that you have released the negative emotional charge from the Root Event, you need to leave the Akashic Plane quickly. Before you leave, visualize[18] and activate the Reiki Mental/Emotional Symbol and embed it into the Heart Chakra of the person you were in the past life memory. This will ensure healing in the memory.

Now, turn around, face the golden light Vortex from which you entered, walk back towards it rapidly, then step into it. In a few seconds, you will feel a sudden pull and instantly you'll be back in your physical body, sitting in the chair. Usually, the return is smooth and effortless, but occasionally you may feel a sudden jerking motion as you return to the chair. Once back in the chair, take a few deep breaths and when you feel ready, open your eyes, and gradually become aware of the room. The session is complete. When you feel ready, get up and stretch. You will find you will be able to recall the entire Past Life Session.

Clearing Psychic Debris

Once you have insight about a Root Event in a past life memory, the negative emotional charge is dispersed, which in turn causes Psychic Debris to be released[19] and healing to begin. The release makes it again necessary to clear the room and yourself after a session. This will ensure any Psychic Debris that has been released is

---

[18] If you are a not a Reiki Healer, go to the next step (i.e., turning around.)

[19] The amount released can vary depending on the individual and his or her condition and circumstances.

destroyed. If the Psychic Debris is not destroyed, it can linger in the room waiting to re-attach itself to you and/or another. It can even negatively affect future events and circumstances that will take place in that room.

Destroying the released Psychic Debris is very simple and should take less than a minute to do. Ask your Source, God, Guides, etc., that all Psychic Debris in the room be dissolved and destroyed. Then visualize white or golden light filling the room and surrounding you. If preferred, use your intent that all Psychic Debris be dissolved and destroyed in the room while bringing the light into the room. If you have time, it also would be helpful to sage or smudge the room.

Stopping a Past Life Session

If you have challenges in viewing a past life memory, try to see the process all the way through. If it becomes too difficult, just end the session, and try again another time. The second session should not be a problem and you will be able to complete the whole process. Please note, if this does happen, end the session as described in the segment *Leaving the Akashic Plan.*

Learn from the past, look to the future, but live in the present.

\- Peter Nemcova

Past Life Session Step-By-Step

An Illustrated Example

This chapter has an example of a Past Life Session with step-by-step illustrations. For demonstration purposes, the session is for an unexplained stomach problem (pain) that has been experienced most of your life – medical doctors cannot find a physical source for the stomach problem.

Past Lives Step-By-Step

1. You have grounded yourself and cleared the room. And now, sitting in a quiet, peaceful place where you will be undisturbed, ask your Source, Higher Self, Guides, Guardian Angels, etc., for guidance during the session (Illus. 21).

2. (If you are not a Reiki Healer, go to step 4.) Draw and activate the Power Symbol in front of the sixth chakra (Third Eye), then visualize it going into this chakra (Illus. 22).

3. Next, draw and activate the Mental/Emotional Symbol in front of the fourth chakra (Heart Chakra), then visualize it going into this chakra (Illus. 23).

4. Silently state the intention and purpose for the Past Life Session in your own words. For example, "I want to discover the Root Event in my past life for my stomach pains and release the negative emotional charge linked to it."

5. Start the Relaxation Technique of your choice.

6. After you are completely relaxed, visualize an almost blinding white or golden light filling the room from the ceiling to floor, slowly spinning, and forming the shape of a Vortex. Take a few moments to view the Vortex (Illus. 24).

Illus. 21

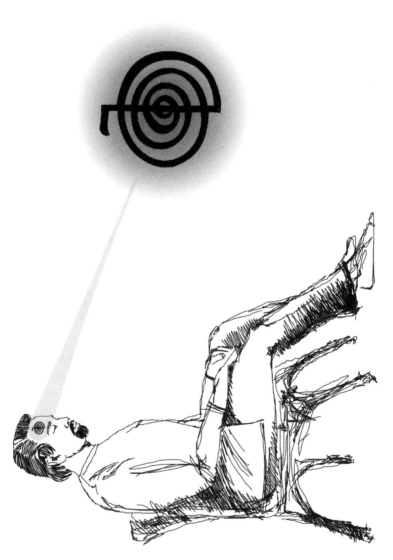

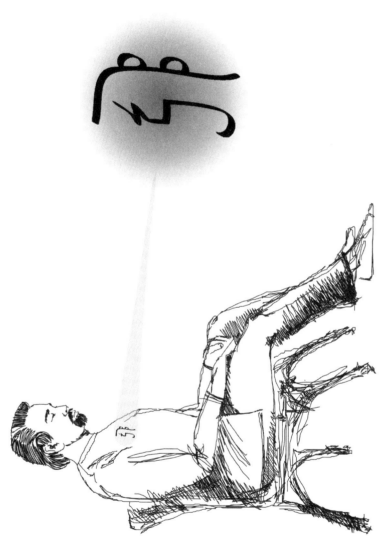

Illus. 23

Illus. 24

7. (If you are not a Reiki Healer, go to step 9.) Draw and activate the Long Distance Symbol, then visualize it going into the Vortex (Illus. 25).

8. Draw and activate the Master Symbol, then visualize it going into the Vortex (Illus. 26).

9. Next, visualize getting up and walking into the middle of this Vortex (Illus. 27).

10. In a few seconds you exit on the other side, and into the Akashic Plane. And in front of you is a flowing grey wall with a porthole (Illus. 28).

11. Take a moment and walk up to the porthole and look in. Looking into the porthole you recognize yourself as a Civil War soldier getting shot in the stomach during a battle (Illus. 29). You see the shock and fear on the soldier's face as he falls backward. Very quickly you understand the soldier has created an emotional charge from this event which has carried over to your present life. With this insight, instantly the emotional charge connected to the Root Event is released in the memory, and it will cease to impact your present life.

12. Once gaining this insight, visualize and activate the Reiki Mental/Emotional Symbol and embed it into the Heart Chakra of the Civil War soldier from your past life (Illus. 30).

13. Now, turn around, facing the Vortex from which you entered, and rapidly walk back into it (Illus. 31).

Illus. 26

Illus. 27

Illus. 28

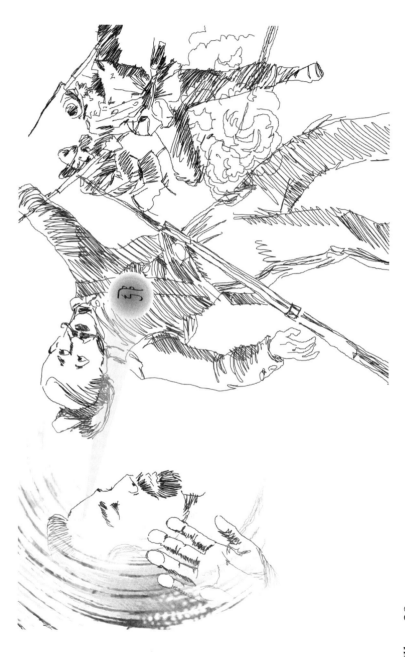

Illus. 30

14. In a few seconds, you will feel a sudden pull and instantly you will be back in your physical body sitting in the chair (Illus. 32). Now, take a few deep breaths and when you feel ready, open your eyes and gradually become aware of the room. The session is complete.

15. Destroy the released Psychic Debris from the session (Illus. 33).

I recommend reading Chapters Seven and Eight and viewing the drawings several times before performing a Past Life Session.

Illus. 32

Illus. 33

I simply believe that some part of the human Self or Soul is not subject to the laws of space and time.

- Carl Jung

Soul Retrieval

Learn the past, watch the present, and create the future.

- Anonymous

Shamans

Shaman Defined

T he concept of Soul Retrieval originates with ancient Shamans. The word *shaman* comes from the Tungus tribe in Siberia and means, "one who sees in the dark." Archaeological evidence has been found that concludes shamanism was practiced all over the world for at least 40,000 years in different cultures. This would make *Shamanism* one of the oldest spiritual practices, if not the oldest, for the human race.

Shamans believed the source of illness was caused by the loss of one's Soul, or part of it. Therefore, the Shaman (Illus. 34) journeyed into the underworld, to the past, or into different worlds/dimensions[20] to retrieve the Soul (or parts of it) and return it to the sick person, thus restoring wholeness and health. How a Shaman retrieved parts of the Soul depended on the Shaman – some talked it back, tricked it back or just dragged it back.

The person the Shaman was doing the Soul Retrieval for laid down next to him and remained passive (sometimes unconscious) during the process (Illus. 35). A Shaman always performed Soul Retrieval in an altered state of consciousness and had various supernatural powers to accomplish the journey successfully. To help enter the altered state of consciousness, the Shaman used a drum or other percussion instruments, such as rattles or sticks, and psychoactive drugs. The supernatural powers were obtained from the Shaman's special guardians, also known as *power animals*.

Various power animals could be summoned as needed during a Soul Retrieval. By doing so, the Shaman could use the animal's unique talent for helping to retrieve the lost Soul and protecting himself, if necessary, during the retrieval. As an example, once in the underworld or

---

[20] Where a Shaman went to retrieve the Soul would depend on the beliefs and the culture of his tribe.

Illus. 34

Illus. 35

other dimension, a Shaman might call upon the powers (tracking, hunting instincts) of a dog (Illus. 36) to help guide him to where the lost part of the Soul is located. Once there, he might need the power (strength, intimidation) of a bear to protect him and help extract the Soul from the location and circumstances where it was found. Next, he could call upon the power (flight) of the eagle to take him back with the lost part of the Soul to unite it with the person who lost it. Usually, the Shaman had his own personal favorite power animals he would use.

The methods I teach for Soul Retrieval will not be as esoteric as the Shaman's methods. You will not be going to the underworld for a part of the soul, nor will you need drumming and psychoactive drugs. In a sense, however, you will learn to be your own Shaman and recover the lost part(s) of your Soul by yourself.

Soul Retrieval

Soul Retrieval is also referred to as *Soul Recovery*. It is a method to recover the part of the Soul that has separated and is left in the past (the reasons for being left will be explained in the next segment), and then uniting it with the rest of the Soul, thereby making the Soul complete and whole again.

This is a very important process for several reasons. When a part of the Soul is missing, it creates a void. Any void in nature needs to be filled. The problem is, this void, on many occasions (perhaps even the majority of the time), is filled mentally, physically or emotionally in the form of mind-numbing substances, food, relationships, addictions,

111

Illus. 36

work, etc. The void filled with Psychic Debris gives a person the feeling of not being whole and signs of Psychic Debris (described in the next chapter) will manifest in the physical body. In due course, Soul separation (loss) causes emotional and physical challenges in a person's life, which will create ongoing stress and eventually a weakening of the immune system.

Soul Fragmentation

I believe the Soul comes into one's current life whole, but a part of it can separate under certain circumstances as you journey through your life. The process of a part of the Soul separating is called "Soul Fragmentation," the term that I will use throughout the book.

Soul Fragmentation can happen during any perceived traumatic circumstance or event in a person's life. I refer to this circumstance or event as an "experience." When the Soul fragments, it is left behind at the place and time of the experience.

A group of people can have the same type of trauma from an experience, yet only one person in the group will have Soul Fragmentation. The reason for this is that every person has a unique life history – how we cope with, handle and perceive circumstances in our lives determines how we will react in any situation, and therefore, what qualifies as "trauma." The type of life stressors undergone prior to the experience in question can also affect whether a Soul Fragmentation takes place. Therefore, an experience that causes a Soul Fragmentation for one person may have the opposite effect on another, by making the Soul stronger.

Soul Fragmentation can occur several ways. One way is if a person experiences an emotional or physical trauma that is so shocking that he or she cannot accept and/or understand the circumstances of the event. When this happens, the trauma is not processed in a healthy manner, mentally or emotionally, to enable the person to cope with it. Sometimes the trauma happens so fast, there is not enough time for acceptance or understanding the occurrence, and the Soul fragments.

A few examples of emotional and physical trauma are loss of a loved one, an automobile accident, surgery, addiction, combat trauma, abortion or miscarriage, all physical and emotional abuse in childhood, sexual abuse, abandonment, or severe illness, debilitation or disease.

On the other hand, the Soul can fragment in a place that you loved or where you felt comfortable and secure (e.g., a grandparent's home that you last visited as a child, before one of them died). And, in some circumstances, your Soul can fragment when leaving a good or bad personal or business relationship (e.g., being fired from a job you loved).

I believe the reason why the Soul fragments is that the Soul compartmentalizes the emotional and/or physical ramifications of a life trauma (situation or event) when the Soul as a whole needs to be protected. Once this is done, the compartmentalized segment is left behind. The reason for this is so that the person can escape or survive the full impact of the emotional or physical pain caused by the circumstance. Another commonly accepted belief is that the Soul fragments automatically every time an emotional or physical event happens, and the size of the fragment depends on how the person perceives the enormity of the event. The large Soul Fragments are the only parts that need to be retrieved.

What does a Soul Fragment look like? In the method I teach, you are going to visualize it looking like yourself when it fragmented. For example, if your Soul fragmented during a traumatic experience when you where a little girl or boy, it will appear as you did at that time.

The present contains nothing more than the past.

\- Henri Louis Bergson

Soul Retrieval

Signs of Soul Fragmentation

To some degree, we all have Soul Fragmentation in our lives, but not every person needs a Soul Retrieval Session. If your life is fine, it is not necessary or recommended to have one. If you have recurring problems[21] in your life, it could be an indication of Soul Fragmentation. The following are just a few signs that could indicate Soul Fragmentation:

➢ Chronic depression
➢ Post-traumatic stress syndrome
➢ Immune deficiency problems
➢ Ongoing grief that will not heal
➢ Addictions
➢ Eyes appear expressionless
➢ Insomnia
➢ Senses are suppressed
➢ Sleeping more than necessary
➢ Apathy towards life
➢ A feeling of not being whole and/or an emptiness
➢ Something missing in life
➢ Lack of childhood memories
➢ Gaps in adult memories
➢ The inability to feel certain emotions
➢ Chronic fears
➢ Chronic illness
➢ Chronic pain

You might have a sign for a Soul Fragmentation and a Root Event problem that are similar; if so, use the following to determine what to do. If you do not recall a traumatic experience in your current life, then a Past Life Session is all that is needed. If you do recall a traumatic experience, do both a Past Life Session and a Soul Retrieval, but perform the Past Life Session first.

---

[21] Problems can be physical, mental or emotional.

Soul Retrieval Session

During a Soul Retrieval Session, you enter the Akashic Plane and access the Akashic Records (past memories) the same as in a Past Life Session. The process of getting to the Akashic Plane will be identical, but there will be three major differences once you are there:

1. Before a Past Life Session, you have no idea what memory you will be accessing beyond the porthole until you view into it. However, before a Soul Retrieval session, you need to know the traumatic experience in your present life that you believe caused your Soul to fragment. This experience will be the basis for your Soul Retrieval.

2. More active participation is needed during the Soul Retrieval Session. You are going to actually enter the current life memory and retrieve the part of your Soul left there.

3. You will leave the Akashic Plane with the lost part of your Soul to reunite with the rest of your Soul.

After a Soul Retrieval

Since we are all unique and our life stories are different, Soul Retrieval results will be varied. The majority of people after a Soul Retrieval do have instantaneous changes; but for others, the changes are subtle and take place over time.

The most common experiences after a Soul Retrieval are feelings of warmth and peace, a new sense of wholeness and well-being. Feelings of joy are often experienced, like the ones felt after being united with a loved one. You can feel energized; all five senses become sharper; and there may be a dramatic shift in consciousness, which includes being in sync with the now. Best of all, any problem that the Soul Fragmentation caused in the current life will subside because the fragment was reunited with the rest of the Soul and Psychic Debris was released.

Soul Retrieval Caveats

When you have signs of a Soul Fragmentation and/or a perceived traumatic experience in your life, it is a good chance that your Soul fragmented during the experience. If during a Soul Retrieval Session you discover your Soul did not fragment during the experience for which you are having the session, just end the session and there will be no harm. This very rarely happens. The majority of the time you will indeed find that your Soul fragmented during the experience for which you are performing the Soul Retrieval Session.

Even though you will learn a technique for entering a current life memory, I strongly urge you not to attempt this during a Past Life Session. This technique should only be used during a Soul Retrieval. To try to bring fragments of the Soul back from a past life memory for fun or curiosity could have unforeseen consequences and complications for the present life, not to mention the possible Psychic Debris that might be acquired. Occasionally, some people have challenges with Soul Retrieval. Most commonly, they think they are ready for a Soul Retrieval Session on the conscious level, but on the subconscious level, they may not be ready to receive the fragment of their Soul back. If this is the case, the person simply will not perform a session until the subconscious mind feels they are ready. In other words, they will never get around to or feel motivated to perform one, no matter how much they may consciously think they are ready.

If you have signs of Soul Fragmentation and are willing to perform a Soul Retrieval Session after reading this book, it will be more than likely that you will be ready for a session on both levels (conscious and subconscious). And, you will ultimately perform a Soul Retrieval Session.

The Present is the living sum-total of the whole Past.
- Thomas Carlyle

Soul Retrieval Nine Segments

Guidance

A Soul Retrieval Session has nine segments. In this chapter, I will explain and guide you though all nine segments. The following chapter will include a sample Soul Retrieval Session with illustrations to help you better understand the process before you perform one.

Nine Segments

➤ Identify the experience
➤ Preparation
➤ Starting the session
➤ Relaxation technique
➤ Entering the Akashic Plane
➤ Insight on why the Soul fragmented
➤ Retrieving the Soul Fragment
➤ Leaving the Akashic Plane
➤ Clearing Psychic Debris

Now we will go through each segment. If you are not a Reiki Healer, omit all the steps that require drawing and activating Reiki Symbols, and go to the next step that does not use a Symbol.

Identify the Experience

Before a Soul Retrieval Session, you need to know the traumatic experience from your current life that you will access during the session. For example, it could be a car accident, a death, a crime, divorce, etc. It will not be necessary to know the exact time, date, year or even the details of the experience for the Soul Retrieval to be effective. It should be noted that an experience is not time sensitive. The experience could have happened just days, weeks or years before a Soul Retrieval Session is performed for it.

Unfortunately, a person might have had several experiences that need to be accessed for a Soul Retrieval. If this is the situation, a session is needed for each experience. Select one experience to begin with, then wait at least a few weeks before performing an additional session for the other experience(s). This gives all of your bodies (physical, mental, emotional and spiritual) adequate time to adjust to a newly reunited Soul Fragment, before retrieving and uniting another.

Preparation

Ground yourself and clear the room before starting a Soul Retrieval Session. All the steps for this are explained in Chapter 4.

Starting the Session

Sit in a quiet, peaceful place where you will be undisturbed for the entire Soul Retrieval Session. As an option, you can ask your Guides, Angels, Source, etc., for guidance and help during the session.

Now draw and activate the Mental/Emotional Symbol above your head, then visualize it going into the Crown Chakra. This will help with the emotional and mental process of the Soul becoming whole again.

Next, draw and activate the Power Symbol above your head, then visualize it going into the Crown Chakra. This will ensure a smooth and fast process of uniting the Soul Fragment with the Soul.

Now, silently state the experience to yourself that you are to access during the Soul Retrieval Session. For example, "I am going to access the memory of when my divorce was final." Use your own phrasing to make it personal.

Performing the Relaxation Technique

Next, perform one of the relaxation techniques explained in Chapter Five. Either one will work. If you have your own relaxation technique that you prefer and it will not make you fall asleep, it can be used.

Entering the Akashic Plane

You are now in a relaxed state. Visualize in front of you an almost blinding white or golden light filling the room from ceiling to floor, slowly spinning, and forming the shape of a Vortex. Take a few moments to view the Vortex.

Now, draw and activate the Long Distance Symbol before you, then visualize it going into the Vortex. This will help with the journey to the Akashic Plane.

If you are a Reiki Master, do the same with the Master Symbol. Draw and activate it, then visualize the symbol going into the Vortex. This helps increase awareness in the Akashic Plane.

Next, visualize getting up and walking into the middle of the Vortex. After a few seconds, you will exit on the other side of the Vortex into the Akashic Plane, a place that is endless and ever-expanding.

You look ahead and in front of you is a flowing grey wall that extends out in all directions as far as you can see, to infinity. You understand the wall is impregnable and represents a veil.

On the wall there is one lone porthole at eye level, and next to the porthole is a door. You know beyond this porthole and door is the fragment of your Soul that you came here to recover, the reason you entered the Akashic Plane. Take a few moments, then when you are ready, walk up to the porthole and look in.

Insight on Why the Soul Fragmented

Looking into the porthole, you will see the memory of the traumatic experience you stated silently to yourself at the beginning of the session.

As in a Past Life Session, you might see images right away. Or, there might be a light, foggy mist or even darkness as you look into the porthole. If this does happen, just keep looking and images will slowly appear. The image(s) might be in natural colors or black and white--whichever way the images appear has no bearing on the process.

Just like in a Past Life Session, when looking through the porthole, several possibilities can happen. You might see images like a short movie and it will play only once, or it will play a few times. Another possibility is you will just see one image that tells the whole story of the traumatic experience.

Once you see (visual) or know (non-visual) the image(s) from the memory, you will instantly recognize yourself. You will appear physically as the age you were at the time in the memory. This image of yourself will represent your Soul Fragment.

The next step is very personal and individualized for each person because every person's experience is different in regard to what happened and why the Soul fragmented. I will give an example in the next chapter that will help you to perform the step, but you need to use your own intuition when performing this step. It has to be that way for the Soul Retrieval to be successful. At this juncture in the session, it's between you and the part of the Soul that separated.

Looking through the porthole, you observe the memory of your traumatic experience with the life wisdom and understanding you have acquired since the experience happened. With the help of that wisdom and understanding, you will gain insight into why the Soul fragmented. Maybe it was for grief, fear, loneliness, protection, etc. The length of time to gain this insight depends on how long it takes to understand why the Soul fragmented. Usually, it requires from a few seconds to a minute, but it can last longer.

You cannot move to the next step until you have this insight. Take as much time as needed for this. Once the insight is acquired, the lost part of the Soul needs to be retrieved.

Retrieving the Soul Fragment

Once the necessary insight is acquired, it is time to open the door next to the porthole and enter the memory to retrieve[22] the lost part of the Soul. Once inside, you will take the Soul Fragment by the hand and lead it back out the door, closing the door behind you as you exit.

The Soul Fragment will always know at a higher level of consciousness why you are there and will come willingly. Some people might want to hug the lost part of the Soul first, or even say a few words[23] before they take the hand and start the journey back. This is a personal preference that will not hinder the process if you choose to do so.

Leaving the Akashic Plane

Now that you have your Soul Fragment by the hand and are outside the closed door, you need to leave the Akashic Plane quickly. Still holding your Soul Fragment's hand, walk towards the Vortex from which you entered the Akashic Plane and step back into it. Once in the Vortex, the Soul Fragment will automatically and simultaneously merge with the rest of the Soul. In a few seconds you will feel a sudden pull, and instantly you'll be back in your physical body. As with a Past Life Session, the return is usually smooth and effortless, but occasionally you may feel a sudden jerking motion as you return to the chair.

---

[22] With some Soul Retrieval Sessions, you may have to carry the Soul Fragment out the door. This could be due to the Soul Fragment having an injury or being a young child. You may consider placing a child on your shoulders before exiting.

[23] Some people might want to tell the Soul Fragment it is safe now, I am taking you home, I missed you, etc.

Now take a few deep breaths, and when you feel ready, open your eyes and gradually become aware of the room. The session is complete. Get up when you feel ready and stretch. You will find you will be able to recall the entire Soul Retrieval Session.

Clearing Psychic Debris

At the end of the Soul Retrieval Session, you need to clear the room of Psychic Debris. Once the Soul Fragment has been reunited, Psychic Debris will be released. This Psychic Debris needs to be destroyed for the same reason[24] as after a Past Life Session and the same method can be used.[25]

Stopping a Soul Retrieval Session

If you have challenges during a Soul Retrieval Session, try to complete the process all the way through. If it becomes too difficult, just end the session and try again another time. The next session should not be a problem and you will be able to complete the whole process successfully. If you must end a session while in the Akashic Plane, make sure you end it as described in the segment "Leaving the Akashic Plane[26]." This is the step of going back through the Vortex into your physical body.

---

[24] Psychic Debris can linger in the room waiting to re-attach itself to you and/or another. It can even negatively affect future events and circumstances that unfold in that room.

[25] See Chapter 8, Clearing Psychic Debris.

[26] Of course, since you are ending the session, you will be going back by yourself, without the Soul Fragment.

The past is not dead. In fact, it's not even past.

- William Faulkner

Study the past if you would divine the future.

- Confucius

Soul Retrieval Session
Step-By-Step

An Illustrated Example

This chapter has an example of a Soul Retrieval Session with step-by-step illustrations. For demonstration purposes, the traumatic experience that comes to mind is when you were a young girl (or boy, if a man), your mother has died, and you realize that she's not coming back.

Soul Retrieval Step-By-Step

1. The traumatic memory (stated at start of the chapter) you are going to access has been decided upon. You have grounded yourself, cleared the room, and you are sitting in a quiet, peaceful place where you will be undisturbed. At this time, ask your Source, Higher Self, Guides, Guardian Angels, etc. for guidance during the session (Illus. 37).

2. (If you are not a Reiki Healer, go to step 4.) Draw and activate the Mental/Emotional Symbol over the Crown Chakra, then visualize it going into the Crown Chakra (Illus. 38).

3. Next, draw and activate the Power Symbol over the Crown Chakra, then visualize it going into the Crown Chakra (Illus. 39).

4. State silently to yourself the memory you are to access during the Soul Retrieval. Use your own phrasing to personalize it. For example, "I am going to access the memory after my mother died."

5. Peform the Relaxation Technique of your choice.

6. After you are completely relaxed, visualize in front of you an almost blinding, white or golden light filling the room from ceiling to floor, slowly spinning, and forming the shape of a Vortex. Take a few moments to view the Vortex (Illus. 40).

Illus. 37

Illus. 39

137

Illus. 40

7. (If you are not a Reiki Healer, go to step 9.) Draw and activate the Long Distance Symbol, then visualize it going into the Vortex (Illus. 41).

8. Draw and activate the Master Symbol, then visualize it going into the Vortex (Illus. 42).

9. Next, visualize getting up and walking into the middle of this Vortex (Illus. 43).

10. After a few seconds, you will exit on the other side of the Vortex, into the Akashic Plane. In front of you is a flowing grey wall with a porthole and a door next to it (Illus. 44). Pause, then walk up to the porthole and look in.

11. Looking through the porthole, you see yourself as a young girl soon after your mother's death, appearing sad and confused (Illus. 45). You know the sadness and confusion stems from the thoughts that your mother has left and is not coming back because she does not love you. With the wisdom and life experience you now have, you understand that you were too young to comprehend life and death, and that your mother did not leave because she wanted to, she did not have a choice in dying, and she always loved you. Once this insight is realized, it's time to retrieve the lost part of your Soul.

12. Open the door next to the porthole and enter the memory. Once inside, take the little girl by the hand (Illus. 46). You can talk or even hug your Soul Fragment whatever you feel intuitively needs to be done before you leave the memory. Next, holding your Soul Fragment by the hand, go back through the door, closing it behind you.

Illus. 42

141

Illus. 43

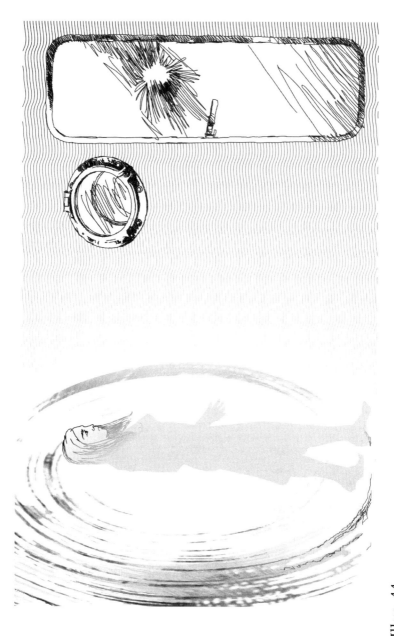

Illus. 44

143

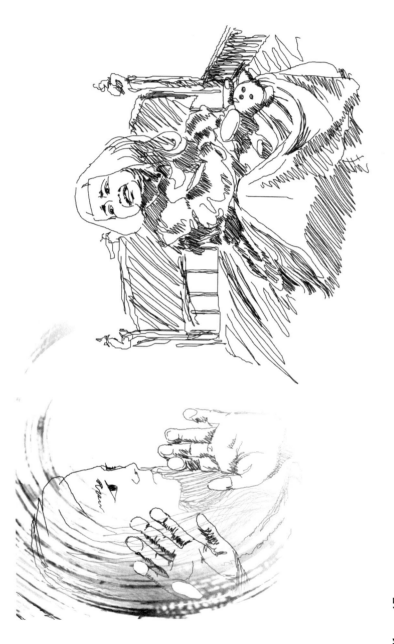

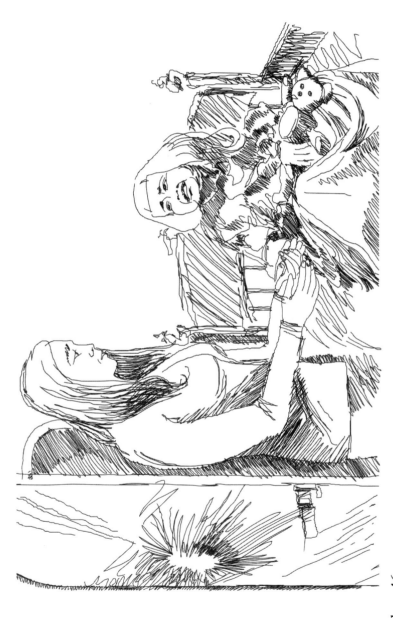

Illus. 46

13. Now that you have your Soul Fragment by the hand and are outside the closed door, you need to leave the Akashic Plane quickly. Still holding your Soul Fragment's hand, walk towards the Vortex from which you entered the Akashic Plane and step back into it (Illus. 47).

14. Once in the Vortex, the Soul Fragment will automatically and simultaneously merge with the rest of the Soul (Illus. 48).

15. In a few seconds, you will feel a sudden pull and instantly you'll be back in your physical body (Illus. 49). Take a few deep breaths, when you feel ready, open your eyes, and gradually become aware of the room. The session is complete.

16. Destroy the Psychic Debris released from the session (Illus. 50).

Read the steps and view the drawings several times before you perform a Soul Retrieval Session.

Illus. 47

147

Illus. 48

Illus. 49

Illus. 50

What lies behind us and what lies before us are tiny matters compared to what lies within us.
- Ralph Waldo Emerson

The past is but the past of a beginning.

- H.G. Wells

Guiding a Session

**The past is a source of knowledge,
and the future is a source of hope.**

- Stephen Ambrose

Guidelines

To Help Others

A relative, friend or client can be guided through Past Life and Soul Retrieval Sessions. The requirements and guidelines for this are relatively simple and can be developed with practice. For simplicity, I will refer to the person being guided through a session as the client.

Requirements

➢ Have a clear voice and patience during a session.

The clear voice is very important so that the client can hear you during the session. Patience is needed because the client will proceed at his or her own pace during the session and you cannot rush them through any step.

➢ Have a complete understanding of all the material in the book.

This will enable you to explain the process to the client and answer any questions about a session. Besides calming the client's fears and doubts on what will take place, an exchange of information will give the client confidence in your abilities to guide a session.

➢ Have the experience of performing Past Life and Soul Retrieval Sessions for yourself.

With experience, you are prepared to guide the client through a session step-by-step without difficulty.

Before a Session Guidelines

➢ Perform the same preparations before guiding a session as you would if you were performing it on yourself – grounding yourself and clearing the room.

➢ Have the client take the visual or non-visual test and explain the reasons for it.

➤ Explain the whole Past Life or Soul Retrieval process to the client so they will know what to expect during the session. This includes the Relaxation Technique used at the beginning of the session. If the Client is also a Reiki Healer, explain how and when the Reiki Symbols will be used during the session. If the client is not a Reiki Healer, symbols will not be used and there is no need to talk about Reiki Symbols.

➤ If it's a Soul Retrieval Session, you need to have the client pick the traumatic experience memory that will be accessed in the Akashic Plane.

➤ Give the client options regarding how to communicate to you during the session when he or she is ready to move on to the next step during the session. It can be verbal, non-verbal (e.g., a nod of the head), or a combination of both. Be aware that a client might decide before the session on a means to communicate, but communicates differently during the session. Just be aware this can happen and adapt with it. It does not make a difference how a client signals they are ready for the next step, as long as you get the message.

➤ Explain to the client they can verbalize what is taking place in the Akashic Plane if they desire, but it is not necessary.

➤ Give the client instructions on how to ground themselves, then guide him or her through the process.

During a Session Guidelines

➢ Stand or sit next to the client while guiding the session. And have the client keep the eyes closed during the entire session.

➢ If the client is a Reiki Healer, he or she can draw the Reiki Symbols at the appropriate time during the session.

➢ Verbalize each step slowly and clearly and tell the client to let you know when the step has been completed. Once the client communicates a step is done, verbalize the next step. Do this with all the steps. It is important your client has completed one step before moving to the next.

➢ During a session, (although rare) the client might become stuck in a step. It will be up to you to find out what the challenge is, talk the client through it, and move the session forward.

➢ If a session cannot move forward, you need to guide the client back from the point of difficulty, and end it.

After a Session Guidelines

➢ After the session is over, it is a good idea to talk to the client talk about what they experienced during the session, but if the client prefers not to talk about it, then do not press the issue.

➢ After discussing the session, while the client is still present, clear the room to remove any Psychic Debris from the room, the client, and yourself.

I would also recommend making an abbreviated (bulleted) list of the steps for the Relaxation Techniques, Past Life Session and Soul Retrieval Session. Use the lists when guiding your first session (or all sessions.) Simply check off each step after the client completes it. In addition to reminding you what each step is, it also helps if you get sidetracked for any reason, so that you will know which step was completed last.

The future is always beginning now.

- Mark Strand

The Future

The Future

The best way to predict the future is to create it.

- Peter F. Drucker

The Butterfly Effect

Manifest a Healthy Future

Once present life challenges are helped by a Past Life and/or Soul Retrieval Session, there is always a concern about the future in a person's life. In this closing chapter, I am going to give you a suggestion on how to manifest a healthy future.

First of all, the future is not carved in stone; it is constantly being altered by Free Will and Causality. Free Will is an individual's personal power and discretion to make decisions about one's life. This is the power that alters your future.

Causality (also known as causation) is the relationship between one event, the *cause*, and another event, the *effect*, which is the result of the cause. The metaphor I like to use for Causality is called the *The Butterfly Effect*.[27] This phrase refers to the concept that a butterfly's wings flapping in one part of the world can ultimately cause a tornado in the future in another part of the world. The flapping of the wings represents a small change in the initial condition of the weather system that causes a domino effect[28] of other additional changes in the weather system leading to the tornado. By the same token, if the butterfly did not flap its wings, another chain of weather events would have occurred. The Butterfly Effect is about weather, but it is an example of Causality and how one event can change the future.

All this means is once you make a Free Will decision (the cause) in your life, it alters your future (the effect). Simply stated, Free Will decisions made on a daily basis directly manifest your future.

Since Free Will and Causality are constants in a complex modern life, you can't dwell upon or worry about every

---

[27] "Butterfly Effect" is credited to Edward Lorenz.
[28] The domino effect refers to a small change which will cause a change nearby, which then will cause another change, and so on. The domino effect also relates to a chain of events.

single Free Will decision made. If you did, you would have never-ending uncertainty and stress in your life. The suggestion I have for this dilemma on Free Will is not new, but it is often neglected and is what all spiritual teachings ask you to do, which is to make sure all Free Will decisions have the intention of the highest good for all, and that includes you.

Decisions made without the intent of the highest good for all have a tendency to manifest future events that are not desired or not beneficial. If Free Will choices and decisions are made with integrity, without doubt or fear, and for the highest good, there is never a need to worry about how a future event will unfold. To make the correct decisions use the following simple formula.

When faced with a Free Will decision, quickly ask yourself what is the choice that would be the highest good for all, and then make the choice that comes to mind and let it go. If you make a choice that gives you an uneasy feeling in your mind and/or physical body, then that's a sign to change the decision to one that will not. The choice that does not give you an uneasy feeling in your mind and/or physical body is always the correct one.

This might be a little time consuming at first, but it will be worthwhile to manifest a healthy future. Eventually, you will program your mind to make the decision for the highest good in seconds and the correct choice will be made and acted upon without hesitation.

Of course, you cannot change the inevitable (i.e., aging or death), but you can alter them. The circumstances on how you age and the time and manner of your death can be altered by Free Will choices made in the present. For instance, if you make the decision not to do some form of exercise now, your body will age faster and be less mobile in the future. On the other hand, choose to exercise and your body will age more slowly and be more flexible in the future. Alternatively, if you have a heart condition caused by diet and do not change your eating habits, the future most likely will be a heart attack. Make a choice to change your diet and the chances of a heart attack fade in the future.

So start right now and alter your future by using your Free Will to choose to make all future decisions with integrity and for the highest good for all.

Shanti,

Steve Murray

Index

Index (continued)

Selected Bibliography

Andrews, Ted. *How To Uncover Your Past Lives.* Llewellyn Publications, 2006. ISBN-10: 0738708135.

Atkinson, William W. *Reincarnation and the Law of Karma.* Cosimo Classics, 2007. ISBN-10: 1602062935.

Bache, Christopher M. *Lifecycles: Reincarnation and the Web of Life.* Paragon House Publishers, 1994. ISBN-10: 1557786453.

Cerminara, Gina. *Many Mansions: The Edgar Cayce Story on Reincarnation.* Signet, 1988. ISBN-10: 0451168178.

Danelek, J. Allan. *Mystery Of Reincarnation: The Evidence & Analysis of Rebirth.* Llewellyn Publications, 2005. ISBN-10: 073870704X.

Ingerman, Sandra. *Soul Retrieval: Mending the Fragmented Self.* Harper SanFrancisco, 2006. ISBN-10: 0061227862.

Johnson, Debbie. *Exploring Past Lives to Heal the Present.* Hushion House Publishing, 2004.

LaBay, Mary Lee. *Past Life Regression: A Guide for Practitioners.* Trafford Publishing, 2006. ISBN-10: 1412012783.

Neff, Joanna. *Soul Retrieval: Return to Wholeness.* Trafford Publishing, 2006. ISBN-10: 1412016134.

Prophet, Elizabeth Clare and Erin L. Prophet. *Reincarnation: The Missing Link in Christianity.* Summit University Press, 1997. ISBN-10: 0922729271.

Shroder, Thomas. *Old Souls: Compelling Evidence from Children Who Remember Past Lives* (Paperback). Simon & Schuster, 2001. ISBN-10: 0684851938.

Selected Bibliography (continued)

Slate, Joe H. *Beyond Reincarnation: Experience Your Past Lives & Lives Between Lives.* Llewellyn Publications, 2005. ISBN-10: 0738707147.

Steiger, Brad. *You Will Live Again: Dramatic Case Histories of Reincarnation.* Revised edition. Blue Dolphin Publishing, 1996. ISBN-10: 0931892295.

Stemman, Roy. *One Soul, Many Lives: First Hand Stories of Reincarnation and the Striking Evidence of Past Lives.* Ulysses Press, 2005. ISBN-10: 1569754691.

Stevenson, Ian. *Children Who Remember Previous Lives: A Question of Reincarnation.* McFarland & Company, 2000. ISBN-10: 0786409134.

Stevenson, Ian. *Twenty Cases Suggestive of Reincarnation: Second Edition.* University of Virginia Press, 1980. ISBN-10: 0813908728.

TenDam, Hans. *Exploring Reincarnation.* Rider, 2004. ISBN-10: 0712660208.

Villoldo, Alberto. *Mending the Past & Healing the Future With Soul Retrieval.* Hay House, 2006. ISBN-10: 1401906265.

Webster, Richard. *Practical Guide to Past-Life Memories: Twelve Proven Methods.* Llewellyn Publications, 2001. ISBN-10: 0738700770.

Weiss, Brian. *Many Lives, Many Masters.* Fireside, 1988. ISBN-10: 0671657860.

Woolger, Roger. *Healing Your Past Lives: Exploring the Many Lives of the Soul.* Sounds True, 2005. ISBN-10: 1591791839.

HOW TO ORDER DVDS, CDS, BOOKS

To buy any of the following Books, DVDS or CDS, check with your local bookstore, or www.healingreiki.com, or email bodymindheal@aol.com, or call 949-263-4676.

BOOKS by STEVE MURRAY

Cancer Guided Imagery Program
For Radiation, Chemotherapy, Surgery
and Recovery

Stop Eating Junk!
In 5 Minutes a Day for 21 Days

Reiki The Ultimate Guide
Learn Sacred Symbols and Attunements
Plus Reiki Secrets You Should Know

Reiki The Ultimate Guide Vol. 2
Learn Reiki Healing with Chakras
plus New Reiki Healing Attunements
for All Levels

Reiki The Ultimate Guide Vol. 3
Learn New Reiki Aura Attunements
Heal Mental and Emotional Issues

Reiki False Beliefs Exposed
For All Misinformation
Kept Secret by a Few Revealed

Reiki The Ultimate Guide Vol. 4
Past Lives & Soul Retrieval
Remove Psychic Debris & Heal Your Life

DVDS by STEVE MURRAY

Reiki Master Attunement
Become a Reiki Master

Reiki 1st Level Attunement
Give Healing Energy to Yourself
and Others

Reiki 2nd Level Attunement
Learn and Use the Reiki Sacred
Symbols

Reiki Psychic Attunement
Open and Expand Your Psychic
Abilities

A Reiki 1st
Aura and Chakra
Attunement Performed

Reiki Healing Attunement
Heal Emotional-Mental-
Physical-Spiritual Issues

Successfully Preparing for Cancer Radiation A Guided Imagery and Subliminal Program

Preparing Mentally & Emotionally For Cancer Surgery A Guided Imagery Program

How To Contact Angels and Departed Love Ones A Step By Step Guide

Preparing Mentally & Emotionally For Cancer Radiation A Guided Imagery Program

Destroying Cancer Cells Guided Imagery and Subliminal Program

Stop Smoking Using Your Unconscious Mind A Subliminal Program

Preparing Mentally & Emotionally For Cancer Chemotherapy A Guided Imagery Program

Lose Fat and Weight Stop Eating Junk! In 5 minutes A Day for 21 Days

Fear and Stress Relief Subliminal Program Let Your Unconscious Mind Do It!

Pain Relief Subliminal Program Let Your Unconscious Mind Do It!

30-Day Subliminal Weight Loss Program Let Your Unconscious Mind Do the Work!

Successfully Preparing for Cancer Chemotherapy A Guided Imagery and Subliminal Program

CDS by STEVE MURRAY

Reiki Healing Music Attunement: Volume One

Reiki Psychic Music Attunement: Volume One

Reiki Healing Music Attunement: Volume Two

Reiki Psychic Music Attunement: Volume Two

Reiki Aura Music Attunement

Reiki Chakra Music Attunement

Cancer Fear and Stress Relief Program

DVDS by BODY & MIND PRODUCTIONS

Learning to Read the Tarot Intuitively

Learning to Read the Symbolism of the Tarot

More of what people are saying...

It is about time that someone had the courage to bring out all the crazy ideas that were spreading around and bring truth to people about Reiki - which is the most wonderful thing in the world. Mr. Murray does that. His carefully written book shows how in truth, Reiki is for everyone. As in all his past books, the content is easy to understand, well formatted and an absolute must for every Reiki Practitioner, and especially every Teacher. *FN*

I have read all four of Steve Murray's Books, Reiki the Ultimate Guides 1, 2, 3, and Reiki False Beliefs Exposed for All. I use them all the time as reference. I have been studying the Healing Arts for some years now and felt my greatest shift in energy when I first took the Reiki One Attunement through Steve's DVD program. Now I am a Reiki Master and I owe it all to Steve Murray's belief that Reiki should be available to all. Without these four books, I would have too many questions and not enough answers. Thank you, Steve! Keep up the good work. I believe you are spreading a powerful peace message to the masses. *MV*

Steve Murray's books and DVDs are wonderful, very informative and easy to understand. I can now give Reiki Attunements to myself and others. I can Beam and Scan, and can protect myself from Psychic Debris. I have read several other books on Reiki in the past, but it was not until after I received the Attunements with Steve Murray DVDs and read Steve Murray's books that I noticed a huge improvement in my skill and I truly felt complete. *WL*

The DVDs were absolutely amazing. The books are excellent and I especially like the repetition of making sure there is an intent before sending Reiki. After reading all the books, I realize that I have been sending Reiki due to the strong intent that I focus. Your books and DVDs are very powerful. Truly, there are no words to describe the power or connection. *TY*

Received Reiki False Beliefs Exposed for All. I could not put it down and I have to say thanks for reinforcing my beliefs. I felt like I was reading a book about my life and struggles through my seven-year journey of Reiki. *SM*

In my opinion this is the best work Steve has done so far, apart from his Reiki Music attunement Vol 1. The music is so well done that it instantly transforms the listener into a different world, which is very tranquil and serene. If you are sensitive to Reiki flow, you can feel that too as soon as you turn on the music. Steve Murray, we want more such music from you in the future. Thank you for this amazing CD. *PC*

Firstly, I must commend you on the wonderful presentation and informative format in which your books and DVDs bring profound understanding and knowledge about Reiki. I especially appreciate the focus you stress on intent during a healing session. The understanding I now have of Chakras, Auras, meridians, and various disorders and how to focus on these healings is priceless. Thank you, thank you, thank you for your open teachings and all the knowledge you bring forward to and for those of us in the healing field and for those considering this option. My gratitude towards you as a Teacher is endless. *BR*

I ordered your DVD just out of curiosity and I found myself surprised. It works! After doing the steps with you, the heat started coming through my hands. I am happily surprised, so I just want to thank you for taking time to do the DVD. I sense Steve to be a humble soul who really wants to share beauty and love. Thank you and I bless you for that. Sincerely, *SA*

After doing the first attunement I was literally walking off the ground. The energy was incredible! Is a Reiki Attunement able to be given through a DVD? YES!! I immediately went ahead and took the next attunement. It's amazing how many friends and family members start lining up once they know you've been attuned! Thanks to the books and DVDs, I was able to channel the energy. I even gave myself the Reiki Aura Attunement for smoking and I'm happy to say that I've been able to drastically cut back! The Master Attunement was the icing on the cake. Steve's attunements are GREAT and I highly recommend that anyone interested in pursuing Reiki Healing read his books and take his attunements. There is no reason to spend hundreds of dollars for an attunement. All anyone needs is Steve Murray's Course (Books and DVDs). *JA*

About the Author

Steve Murray is the author of the best selling **Reiki The Ultimate Guide** series, and has a series of self-healing programs on DVD. The DVD subjects include Reiki Attunements, Cancer Guided Imagery, weight loss, pain, fear, and stress relief, just to name a few. He has produced six Reiki CDs for healing, meditation, Aura, Chakra and psychic sessions.

Steve is an experienced Usui Reiki Master, but one of his most powerful Attunements came from the High Priest of the Essene Church, which made him an Essene Healer. The Essenes have been healers for more than 2,000 years. Steve is also a Hypnotherapist and a member of the National League of Medical Hypnotherapists and National Guild of Hypnotists.

"Shanti" **Steve Murray**